Thirty Shades of GrAyton:

A single girls' guide to navigating the most perilous road in a one road town!

Acknowledgements

Before we start this trip together, I would love to give credit to some very special and talented people: Lisa Burwell and her team at the Idea Boutique, for all sorts of literary insight. And to Dawn Chapman Whitty for such beautiful photos- it's only fitting since you shot my wedding...To Sean Murphy for catching my sporty side HA!! To my parents, children and siblings- blood relatives or otherwise- Thank you for being my unwitting therapists and never-ending supply of love and support! You all know who you are. You are my inspiration! Thank you all for teaching me to never again hold my peace! Alright! Let's get this party started!

Foreword:

Breakups are never easy. Small town breakups are exceptionally painful and awkward. I remember being so pleased that this was never going to be a subject on which I would become an expert. So certain I was that I would never be thirty something and single! After all, I had been married to a handsome, loving and attentive man for my entire adult life. My children and family were idyllic and my man LOVED the heck out of me! But then, ever so suddenly, there I was so single and so inexperienced! I hadn't been on a proper first date in thirteen years! When it came time to pick up the pieces and put myself out there, I began to realize quickly that small town dating can be a strange and wondrous thing!

My family lives in a quaint town located on some of the most beautiful beaches in the world. The main artery of this small town is a scenic road known as 30A. My family business resides in a sweet little village called Grayton Beach. Known for its nice dogs and strange people, Grayton has long been at the center of my life. It is where I met my husband, where we got married, where we worked, where our children met all of the people who would help us shape their lives. Everyone knows everyone. And everyone is connected in one way or another. This very connected, very tuned in home is where I found myself suddenly single, suddenly very interesting, and suddenly forced to start anew.

So I did it. I didn't just jump into a new life… I have never liked free falls. But I closed my eyes, held my breath, and stumbled in feet first. I stood out like a baby giraffe on an ice rink, but I did it! Along the way I experienced so many strange new things. I had so many valuable conversations with other single people. I connected with so many new friends and I have learned a lot about what a small town single has to deal with. I began to think that I could put together a plan to make this new life a little easier, a little sillier and a lot more fun. I think of the bits of my life that I choose to share as my personal shades. Shades of wisdom from a startled single lady! I've never been accused of being appropriate and I warn you, some of my stories are, let's just say brash. I'm learning that I like to live with a certain lack of filter. I hope that if you are reading this you will be able to learn, laugh, and grow with me. My shades are ever changing as should yours!

***

Build a ladder from your broken bits. Climb it to dance on bars, swing from chandeliers, and rise to be the biggest bad "A" in your life! Remember who you are, who you wanted to be, and, Babe, make it happen! The whole world is your 30A. Take it wherever you go. Be your best 30 Shades and own each and every one!

Kyle Petit

1. All Paths Lead to Grayton

This is my longest chapter, I promise. But I just thought that we might get to know each other before going all the way. I'm not from Grayton. Hardly anyone is actually from Grayton. No, I grew up in a small town far, far away. My winters were snowy and my summers were spent on the river that ran through my back yard. I was a very peculiar child. I'm not afraid to admit that. I loved to be alone. I cherished my time in the woods playing with the fairies and other creatures that I created in my mind. I was an outdoorsy, sporty girl named Kyle with a haircut crafted by my father's barber. Even Mr. Tremont, the barber, assumed that I was a boy until the day that I showed up with my Strawberry Shortcake kicks on. This made it particularly awkward for me when I was made to wear a dress each Sunday! My closest friends were a few boys from the neighborhood, a tomboy girl from the farm across the street, and some interesting adult neighbors. I recall one neighbor in particular who had travelled the world. They had one of those houses where the décor consisted of artifacts collected from the places they had seen.

This is where my path started. I used to sign cards with a footnote to hold on to them because some day I would rule the world! I was destined for Greatness! As it turns out I was simply destined for Grayton. Looking back, I can map my journey to here in ten easy steps.

Step 1: Learning about faraway places. I was six years old the first time that I tasted Brazilian cow tongue and black beans at my eclectic neighbors' home. The mother there was an opera singer and the father was in the import business. The stories that they would weave about their adventures opened my eyes to a whole world that was just waiting for me to see.

Step 2: Learning to speak. By age seven I was convinced that I needed to learn how to speak French and Spanish. So convinced was I that my poor parents could never hear the end of my dreams of castles and mountains and ships. One day a lady whos name I will never recall offered to start an after school program teaching one semester of French and one of Spanish. Funny that I can't remember her name, because I owe this woman my life. As it turns out, the human brain begins to lose its capacity for learning new languages at age twelve. Which is precisely that age at which we, as Americans, are offered foreign language in most public schools. Imagine that a door starts to shut at that age, but you can put a stopper on it if you are introduced to multiple languages before the door starts to close. It was thanks to this program that I am now fluent in not one but three languages, and I can pick up and converse in many others.

Step 3: Divorce. In the fifth grade, my parents filed for divorce. This is a game changer in anyone's life. It made my life at the time extraordinarily tumultuous. My parents didn't handle each other very well and home life was difficult. I must say, having experienced this myself as an adult, that there is no good way to handle the kind of heartbreak that comes from the end of one life, but this end propelled me to a new beginning.

Step 4: Waterskiing and Jimmy: As I mentioned, I grew up on a river. Our weekends were spent on the boat skiing and listening to Jimmy Buffett. As things at home grew difficult, my parents sought out an activity that would be my means of escape from the tension. A nearby town had a waterski show. The Aquanuts in Twin Lakes, Wisconsin saved my life! For me it was ski or flee! The team gave me a safe haven and a sense of purpose that I desperately needed. They also had a healthy respect for Jimmy Buffett. I remember so clearly the nights that I would fall asleep at a team mates house listening to “A Pirate looks at Forty” or “He Went to Paris”, dreaming of all of the places I would go. Imagine my father’s joy upon hearing his youngest daughter belt out “Why don’t we get drunk and screw”! Jimmy made me dream of beaches and sun and lands unknown. Jimmy was a big part of my path.

I'll just leave it there before I give my inner Parrothead away completely.

Step 5: Home EC... Really? This peculiar child became a most peculiar teen and when Middle school rolled around I was very eager to resume my language education. But, how to choose? I couldn't choose between my aptitude for Spanish and my dream of seeing France! I had two electives available to me, but only one could be a foreign language! My other options were shop or home economics. Really? Home EC? I was destined for greatness, not sewing a pillow in the shape of a K (a feat which I later taught myself on my mom's machine- her bobbin would never recover). Needless to say, I petitioned the school board to allow me to take both Spanish and French simultaneously. Thanks to some very patient teachers, and one brilliant coworker form Mexico, I placed sixth in the national Spanish exams with only two years under my belt. Hey, some people do math... I do grammar and syntax.

Step 6: Peru, no Spain, no FRANCE! By the time this peculiar girl was seventeen, I was ready to make a break. A few academic successes and some strong foreign language capacity lead me to the Rotary Youth Ambassador scholarship. I once again found myself petitioning the school board. This time I was fighting for my right to graduate a full year early so that I could head off to parts unknown. I owe the Rotary my life, both metaphorically and quite literally. My scholarship first landed me an ambassadorship in Peru. At the time my Spanish was better than my French and I was elated to have the chance to see such an amazing country. Fate intervened in the form of political unrest. The Rotary decided to send me to Spain instead. Europe!!! That magical land beyond that had called to me since I was so young was finally within reach. Fate showed her hand again, this time in the form of a terrorist act on a train. This led me to France. I finally landed in a town very near the fabled Provence. Lavender and sunflowers, mountains and rivers were my new every day. I was in love, my soul finally home, and I embraced every amazing breathtaking moment of my life in my own personal paradise. I was so in love with the country, the language, and the people that I never stopped for a second to think that I would have to one day say goodbye. France will always be home to my spirit. It is where I felt for the first time that I was truly alive. Like Redbull, France gave me wings. I had only one plan and that was to find my way back.

Step 7: College and Internships aka "Dude, that was fun!" College in the US started at the University of Illinois, and continued on at the University of Kansas. Pledging GDI gave me plenty of time to devote to my favorite subject: the waterski team. Mind you, I was still very interested in my major subjects, French, Spanish, and Italian. And I did manage to get a few more scholarships to help me out along the way. My weekends consisted of campouts and tournaments, and my weeks were work and school. Hands down some of the greatest days of my life! Nearly every summer I had a job or internship that required me to use my languages. I just knew for sure that this was my path. I would finish school and go to work for some corporation as a translator in a cubicle in some high rise in Paris or Madrid. Eventually I would make enough money to buy a small bed and breakfast in the Alps where I would meet some dashing millionaire skier and live out my days in childless, passionate harmony. That was not meant to be.

Step 8: Waterskiing again! Ever since I had started to take my sport seriously, I had dreamed of being one of those awesome people that lives for a summer at the ski school working and teaching in exchange for room and board and water time. My last summer in college brought with it the opportunity to be a cook in the best ski school in the world. Every one of my bunk mates was a rock star in the sport! I have always loved to cook and ski, and here was my chance to do both. That summer there were thirty staff and students from all over the world living together at the bunk house we called Home. The majority of my mates were from Central and South America. I spent the first couple of months pretending that I couldn't understand them when they would talk about the "bikini chef" in Spanish. "Oh she's mopping the floors in a swimsuit again... or haha she's chopping veggies in her bikini!" It wasn't until they insulted my cooking one afternoon that I unleashed the full extent of my vocabulary upon them. Fifteen handsome Latin jaws hit the floor, and once they asked me when I had learned to speak their language I replied, "Ayer baby!" Hehe that has to be one of my favorite moments ever!

Step 9: My other path. One of the instructors at the ski school that fateful summer was a fellow from Belgium. He and I bonded over the fact that he didn't have to speak English with me. This man would change my path forever. Looking back, I'm pretty sure that he was trying to take me on a date when he offered to introduce me to another friend from Belgium, but I have long had a rule that I will not date a waterskier. Just a personal choice, nothing against all of those hunky boys- they are easy on the eyes. I just didn't want to date anyone for a season and that kind of sin is only good for a season! That said, on that very night my bunkmate inadvertently introduced me to the man that I would marry not even one year later.

Step 10: Grayton. That night, my Belgian friend took me to Grayton. My favorite restaurant and bar was our destination. You see he knew the owner, a handsome young man who seemed very happy to meet a young lady who could speak his native tongue. I will never forget the first time I saw him. How could I? He was so tall and handsome and tongue-tied. He kept coming up to me to grab my face saying "You're so pretty, and you speak French!" I remember clearly thinking that what he lacked in conversational skill he made up in raw charm. Ten months later, and seven months preggo, that charming- and as it turns out easy to talk to man made me his wife. Right there in Grayton on the beach with a jazz band processional and killer sunset backdrop. This man would give me two stepdaughters, a son and a baby girl. He introduced me to the family business and ignited in me a passion for food, service and people. I was happy. It turns out that all of my studies, all of my interests, all of the parts of my master plan had lead me right here to Grayton. They had lead me to this Belgo-Italian entrepreneur with Costa Rican in-laws. The call of the World was dulled by the cries and laughter of my sweet babies and the adoring words of my husband. We were happy, until we just weren't. Never good at timing, he left me the morning after our anniversary. May thirteenth, 2013, in the thirteenth year of our relationship- poof! He was gone. I vowed to never bet on 13 and I took my first steps onto my new path. Suddenly single in a very small town, my new life would begin with the lessons that I learn every time I head out on our beloved 30A. Or the "A" as I like to call it. I will refer to the "A" throughout this guide, but you have your own 30A and the same rules still apply!

2.Teasy to Easy

So, you're finally single; remember that you have just gone from teasy to easy! Small towns have a mega shortage of "fresh blood". If you are newly single, and especially if you have never been on the local market, you will attract a lot of attention from men who are just DYING to meet the new girl!

Pace yourself and be DISCREET! All eyes are on you in this moment. You are the shiny new toy and everyone wants to play. You don't necessarily need to give people more to discuss. Take this one from me, ladies, I learned it the hard way. Being left behind often leads to the feeling that you are no longer desired or desirable. The attention is flattering for sure and awesome for that big ole bruise on your ego, but you need to protect your little broken heart.

When dating on-as we call it- the "A", keep in mind that the gentleman sitting across the table from you has dated or slept with one, or all, of your single girlfriends. My advice; skip the small talk, text a gal-pal and find out how this evening will go! Small town dating is an incestuous affair. If this were New York, I could probably avoid run-ins with my ex and his whoever. Instead, I seem them daily. They are everywhere, a constant reminder of what I failed to protect! Worse, they know, see or hear about ALL of my extracurricular activities and I get the added pleasure of hearing about theirs. Since it is a small town, when your ex moves on, you will know her pretty well. Awkward is the only word for this.

Other awkwardness can arise if you are not extremely rigorous in the background investigation of prospective dates. Seriously ladies, Google a dude! I know a girl whose first lunch date ended with months of cyber-stalking and textual harassment at the hands of a convicted offender! I'm not saying that it was me, but YIKES! Just take a moment to check. No matter how good he looks in his mug shot, this, my dears, is a man to avoid! Aren't we already kinda sold out on crazy?

*** Side note: Any men who may have decided to venture down the proverbial rabbit hole and read this guide, please pay attention! No woman in the history of womankind has ever needed, or for that matter, wanted a self-portrait of your male member sent via text, IM, or messenger. Keep it in your pants boys! Leave a girl something to the imagination. We all know how proud you are of your manliness, we just don't need photographic evidence! At the very least please wait until she has seen it in person and approved ;).

3.Taking Your "A" off the "A"

Anyone who has dated in a small town can tell you that you see a lot of the same old faces in the same old places. It can begin to feel like "Groundhog Day" and that damned Punxsutawney Phil is never gonna step out of his box! Ladies- and gentlemen- If you do not take some time away from the "A" to broaden your prospective horizons, you will probably blow through all of the interesting local possibilities in under a year. And, truly I say to you, you do not want to be the person who slept with the entire "A" in under a year! Guys, this makes you a player. Ladies, this makes you a slut. This is a double standard that we will address a little further down the road. I know it's not fair, but it is a reality that we all must recognize.

Dating tourists does NOT count as taking your "A" off the "A"! Even if he's a new face, it's still the same old place. Everyone has done it! The temptation is too great! An easy, fun week with someone from somewhere that's not here sounds perfect. However, people are still people and the 30A is still the "A". People talk, people watch and people judge.

In an effort to keep my private life, well, private, I decided to venture off the "A". I started to resent the feeling of constant gossip swirling all around me. Apparently when a mother becomes single in a small town, she is expected to stay at home, give up, and grow old mourning the loss of her glory days. I'm not that kind of mama. I spent the entirety of my twenties raising up babies. Babies that I adore, but babies who are little no more. I still deal with feelings of inadequacy as a parent while trying to allow new possibilities into my life. I didn't need people making me feel worse... So I went AWOL from the "A". This break from scrutiny was just what I needed! I highly recommend the occasional field trip to a town nearby. It is amazing what freedom comes when you are not playing the lead in the local "Days of our Lives". And you will be surprised at how refreshing it is to meet someone new, who doesn't know your story and just would like to know you better. After all, it is hard enough to move on after a love is lost, don't star in anyone else's stories just go and make your own!

I'm not trying to suggest that living in a small town is an unending stream of gossip and judgment. Well, I'm not trying to suggest that there isn't more to it than that. I feel that I must take a moment to add that I am grateful that I can hug the necks of everyone in town on any given Sunday, and that if I miss church or the beach for too long, people care enough to see if my family is alright. My friends and I check in with one another regularly and I never feel alone. You don't get that in a big city. You don't get that with anonymity. And I wouldn't trade my small town for anywhere else in the world!

4.Tindervention

As I mentioned in the foreword, I was in a relationship for thirteen years before finding myself single. The last time I was out there in the world on my own, there was no Facebook, there was no Insta-anything, no Tinder or other phone apps. Hell, I didn't even OWN a cell phone the last time I was a free woman! If I wanted to watch porn, I had to get HBO or Skinamax like everyone else. It is literally a whole new world out there for the likes of me. This time around I am surrounded by the possibilities presented through social media. An app like Tinder can be riotously funny if you are on it in a tourist town after the boys of summer have all gone!

The moment you realize that these social apps are doing more harm than good, stage an immediate "Tindervention"! If you see a friend that is in need of a Tindervention, help a sista out! It's hard to recognize the power that social media can have over your life when you're the one behind the screen. I have friends that have been in need of such actions. Some are just going on way too many dates, jumping from one empty scenario to another. Some are striking up full blown relationships with a person who may or may not really exist. It's easy to fall for someone who is only sharing the best of themselves through an electronic means of communication.

The previously mentioned Tindervention is actually not just applicable in a small town. People everywhere, all over the world, should try to step out from behind the screen and practice real interpersonal interaction. That said, small town social media is a whole other animal. My personal Tindervention came just a mere sixteen hours after I created my account. I noticed that I already knew personally about ninety percent of the gentlemen (I use that term loosely, like when I call myself a lady) that were being presented for me to like or swipe left. I actually went ahead and "liked" a couple of my real life friends and texted them later that they must understand that I was pulling a funny. If any of these people were remotely interested in me they had ample opportunity to express it on any of the nearly seven days a week we see each other. Any given Friday night these emotions could have been expressed in real time. Even if a declaration of love sounds like you have peanut butter stuck to the roof of your mouth after one too many fireball shots, if it was meant to happen it would have long before I resorted to social media. Disheartened and, honestly, a little wierded out, I closed my account for good. No trace of a single woman named Kyle remained. She was never there, lost forever to the ether.

***Side note: Beware of *Catfish*! It is easy to create an online persona using fake details and photos. Wasn't there a football player whose dying girlfriend was really just some douche nozzle dude pretending to be a girl online? It's cruel and crazy but there is a nozzle born every day. Do not allow yourself to be taken in by these posers!

5. Taxi Cab Confessions

When one lives in a town that really only has one road, a good cab driver can be a single gal's best friend. My favorite cab driver has seen me at my best and at my very, very worst. He was the first to surmise my new singledom and the first to see my baby steps towards moving on. Your cab driver, should you develop a relationship with one, will prove to be your sometimes savior, your in-a-pinch alibi, and your forever good friend. Your cabby will be the first to know your sorrows. He or she will also be the first to know your joys. And with a little luck, he will be your confessor keeping all that he sees and hears confined to the walls of his trusty cab.

If you are lucky enough to live in a small town, your cabby will likely know everyone well enough to gently steer you away from poor decisions, and sometimes give you a nudge in the right direction. These "nudges" may not only save your reputation, but they may also save your life. No one, for any reason, should ever hop behind the wheel intoxicated. We all know this. Our DARE officer sent the message home in the fourth grade, and if that didn't do the trick, that gruesome video from Driver's Ed probably did.

Here are some things that a small town taxi driver might have the joy of experiencing:

1. Learning how to decipher slurred speech: This a very special talent! And I consider myself a linguist. Imagine trying to understand an address being delivered by an over-served mouth! One too many Fireball shots and BAM your speaking a whole new language!
2. Excessive PDA: You all know who you are! At one time or another we have all forgotten

ourselves in the back seat of a cab. Locking lips with some random- or not- hottie –or not- completely ignorant of the very sober very aware witness behind the wheel.

3. Temporal dysfunction: A complete lack of awareness of the passage of time on behalf of the inebriated passenger. A call for a taxi at midnight may very well lead to an actual passenger arrival at twelve fifteen, as the passenger may be spending extra time hugging each and every person in the establishment on her way out (Small town probz, you know everyone at the bar)! The passenger may also be too busy busting out on the dancefloor to hear the phone ring when the taxi arrives.
4. This is a BIG NO NO: Lack of fare. While I am certain that no one ever does this intentionally, it is never alright to not pay your taxi driver. If you are not certain that you will remember to snag some cash at the end of the evening, stop by an ATM on your way out, put at the very least a $20 bill in a

side compartment of your wallet and make sure that you are covered!

5. Witnessing cougars in their natural habitat: These sightings are most often reported by taxi drivers and bartenders on ladies night. A cougar is often lured out by discounted drinks and the musical stylings of Journey, and/or Poison

All of these wonderful perks to the job are exactly why I personally feel that there should be a National Safe Ride holiday. There should be a day set aside for us to recognize the importance of the service that these brave men and women provide. There is only one flaw in this lofty plan; who will give them a ride home from the party?

The Single Earring Club

Own it sisters! The topic of taxis has lead me to this. Since I have been single on Thirty A, I have noticed that I am leaving earrings in bars, cabs, couches, and yards all over town. Invest in some post earrings or those little rubber tubie things that come with the chandelier style ear accessory.

6. Beyond the Small Town Probz:

I have spent a bit of time pondering some of the general pitfalls of dating that may reach far beyond my sweet little Thirty A. I don't want to brow beat any of us ladies and gents, but we ALL make mistakes that could easily be avoided if we can heed a bit of sound advice. I have had to learn some of these lessons the hard way, and some by simply observing a train wreck in action. You don't have to take any of this seriously, that's a free will kind of thing. However, I wouldn't be able to sleep at night without passing these particular shades of wisdom along. Just three simple notes that can save oh so much heartache, frustration and embarrassment. Clearly I don't take my self too seriously, but this stuff is IMPORTANT. If I can make life easier for even just one of you, this journey will have been worth it!

1. Say what you mean, and mean what you say: This is so critical. Ladies, A man almost always means exactly what he says. It's the way that they communicate. They are hardwired to be direct. If he says that he will call you tomorrow, he does not mean that you should call him twenty five times before he gets the chance to dial. If he says that he does not want a serious relationship, he means just that. If you are looking for something more, find another man. If you are only interested in companionship, just say so. Men don't speak in riddles, they don't think in shades of gray. This is a black and white situation and the sooner you understand this the better.
2. If you want a real relationship, STOP HOOKING UP WITH YOUR FRIENDS! There is nothing wrong with having a friend with benefits. I actually highly recommend this practice, as long as you and your bed buddy are on the same page. Having a bed buddy can fulfil your physical needs while keeping

your number of conquests to a minimum. However, when the time comes that you are feeling like taking it further, your buddy will most likely still be wanting to keep it cool. Just be honest with him and should he not desire more from your relationship, move on before you burn any bridges. Sexual compatibility is a beautiful thing and you don't want to write your friend off completely in case you ever want to redeem those benefits at later date!

3. Beware the cat who came back! If you have ended a situation with your "buddy" due to your want of a deeper relationship, try your hardest to stay away. If your friend has bruised your ego in any way and you are not on the same page, you will surely end up hurting again. My advice; think long and hard before you decide to let him back in the saddle. And if you have been drinking you may feel especially vulnerable. This is a time to avoid your former bed buddy at all cost!

7. Friend Zone

We all have at least one. That really cute guy, who is dependable, easy going, so totally perfect for you, and so stuck being your friend. Having a friend zoner is an unavoidable part of single life. You may find yourself confiding in this man in ways that you would not confide in your lover. Your friend offers a safe place where you are never judged and eternally adored. Please, please be honest with your doomed friend! Do your best to never lead him on. DO NOT sleep with him –unless y'all fall asleep on the couch watching "The Golden Girls" or some other chick media on a rainy Friday night. This is paramount. You can sleep with any Joe on the street, but real friends are irreplaceable and sex in the friend zone causes much pain and confusion. Also... you never know when you're gonna need a tire changed!

Slip-ups happen. It is so easy to blur the line between closeness with a member of the opposite sex and genuine attraction. Not that this has ever happened to me, but if you ever find yourself a little buzzed and making out like a teenager with your “friend zone” in the parking lot of the only late night bar in town, gently remind him that this is as far as the romance is going.

It needs to be noted that your gay boyfriend does not count as a friend zoner. A poor fellow only finds himself in the zone if he is attracted to you. If you are lucky enough to have a GB, never give him up! He may very well be the only man in your life who will be truly honest with you. Face it, your father loves you too much to see clearly, and your lover simply wants to find his way back into bed. Often brutally honest, the GB will be a voice of reason cutting through the hormonal fog that is your dating world. He will tell you if your man is hot enough and if your dress is short enough. His opinion will be more objective than any of your girlfriends’ since these gals may be unwittingly competing with you for available men.

8. Grace Periods

Let me define: A grace period is a small town break-up staple. Specifically, a grace period refers to the amount of time that a couple in a small town should avoid contact upon breaking up. This is a sticky point. The last time that I found myself single, there was no need for a grace period. My ex-beau and I were from different social circles on a very large college campus. Avoiding each other was easy!

That said, you can imagine my annoyance at recently having a grace period imposed upon me by a man I had been "talking" to. We parted ways peacefully and as friends. What I expected was that we would remain in close contact, but just not sleep together. I mean easy peasy, right? Not so: he insisted that we needed some time apart in order to settle our mutual attraction and emotions. I was floored! But in the end, he was absolutely right. It's a small town. He was everywhere and so was I. Seeing each other in public was alright. Groups of friends always offer a welcome distraction from any awkwardness. But if we had kept up with the texting, calling, and general one on one time... he could have easily been the cat who came back. Grace periods are not easy. Especially if you truly value your friendship with the person that you are supposed to avoid. After all, you get used to the every - day contact with someone who makes you laugh harder than anyone else, who thinks your brand of weird is cute, who is amazing in the sack, and who just gets you in general. Cutting that off cold turkey can feel like losing a limb. Yet grace periods are a good thing. The time apart allows the dust of your fallen relationship to settle.

Grace periods have rules. As with everything in life, following a few simple guidelines will make your situation infinitely more agreeable. Check out these simple steps to a successful grace period...

1. Lose his number: I put this one on the top of the list for so many reasons, not the least of which is that a few drinks can lead to some very embarrassing text messages and phone calls. You all know what I'm talking about! I can't be the only one to have fallen victim to the late night impulse to drunk dial, or schwasty text! Do yourself a HUGE favor and lose his digits. You will not only avoid embarrassment and awkwardness, it will also spare you both any confusion that may arise if communication continues.
2. Unfriend him on Facebook: It's a grace period ladies! In a small town you're bound to be kept up to snuff on his comings and goings. Concerned friends will always be sure to keep you informed. Besides, what else is

there to talk about? Don't torture yourself by trolling his Facebook page. You are supposed to be moving on and seeing the pictures of him out with the boys, or maybe even a new girl, is not going to help this process. After all, who he went to watch the game with should no longer be your concern. I only offer this advice because I have seen it all too often. Gals get hooked on keeping tabs on their ex partners via social media. This is unhealthy. How do you get over it if you can't get off his page? If you are concerned about hurting any feelings, just explain to him honestly that you feel that unfriending is an important part of your process- that it's just as much to his benefit as it is yours. Put the ball in his court. How can he be expected to get over *you* if he can't get off *your* page?

3. DO NOT STALK HIM!!!!: This should be a given. I should not even have to mention this, yet here we are. I get it, you miss him. You really miss him. Even if your break up was mutual, or even your idea, losing contact with someone with whom you had good chemistry can be awful. Although it won't go on forever, this grace period can feel like an eternity. Stalking him is the one sure-fire way to guarantee that you will never again be friends. Not only is it rude, it can be downright scary for the object of your obsession. I know it's a small town, but if you end up at the same place, make sure that it is only by happenstance. You know him well enough to know his social habits, maybe arrange your social schedule to avoid some of his regular spots on his regular days. Also avoid driving through his neighborhood. Who

cares what kind of car is in his driveway? What good can this knowledge do for your emotional state? When it comes down to it, this person was your friend. Would you want to scare and generally disquiet a friend? Would you want someone to reciprocate these actions upon you? Clearly your intentions are not malicious, but the result of your lack of control can be disastrous. We are how we treat each other right? If you wish to come out on the other end of this grace period with the respect and understanding of your friend, treat him with respect and understanding.

Follow these simple shades of advice and you should have a very pleasant grace period. After enough time passes, if you can maintain a healthy respect for the boundaries that you both have set, you should be able to be friends. That is to say that you should be friends again unless one, or both, of you is a complete douche nozzle.

9. **Happiness in My Pants!**

Now that we have been together through eight of my shades, we should make it official. It's time to take a short side trip off the reservation. Let's face it ladies, no matter what your mama told you- your happiness lies squarely in your oh so capable hands. No man, woman, or child can make you truly happy. Only you can do this. You have to be in charge of your emotional well-being. Of all the things that we desire to control in life- jobs, relationships, destiny, etc... Your emotional and physical states are really the only two things that you can directly influence through the power of sheer will.

A man can put a smile on your face. A man can put happiness in your pants. Having a lover can cast a rosy glow over all the world. It can make your small town feel like the French Riviera in May. Every day could possibly be Valentine's Day. You may feel that there is nothing that this man can't do. Listen up! This is your deepest self about to speak… That rosy tingly feeling is your pituitary gland in overdrive. This man may be really amazing in so many ways, but he cannot make you love yourself. And, sometimes, the more you love him the less you remember *how* to love yourself.

This is where we leave the reservation… Ahem… You do know that you, too, can make your own brand of happy, right? Personal love is such a taboo for American women. This is so sad because it is such an important part of really knowing what will satisfy you physically. Small towns are full of moms who relate sex with sin, and view personal exploration as an absolute NO. Please take this shade from one previously repressed woman to another; personal love can make your pants happy and put a smile on your face.

This is your body! You should write the manual on how it works. There are different strokes for different folks, and each of us should take the time to figure out what makes us tick. I'm not here to tell you how to do it, that's entirely up to you. I, personally, learned a lot on the internet. There are plenty of sites that have video material- if you catch my drift. The fun lies in experimentation!

BONUS The more that you can learn about making your own pants happy, the more fun you will have with a partner. A healthy knowledge of personal satisfaction will also make you less eager to find you next new "toy", protecting both your health and your reputation.

10. She's a Ten

When dating in a small tourist town, you aren't simply competing with your hot, single girlfriends for local affection. No, as if that weren't hard enough- and I mean it, ALL of my girlfriends are HOT- you are also in competition with an unending ebb and flow of uninhibited women on vacation. Picture a beach full of 'em! Each and every one a ten. Blondes, brunettes, and gingers, each one is hotter than the last. They are busty, curvy, skinny, and rich. These chicas are thirty shades of sexy and they go on parade after every spectacular sunset at local watering holes.

These women have money. Beach vacations are not cheap. We have already established that they are smoking hot. With streakless spray tans, recently touched up roots and over-worked personal trainers, these tourists are a force to be reckoned with. Add to the mix that they are usually slightly wasted and ready to make bad decisions while away from partners, and the situation becomes dire. There seems to be a never-ending, rotating smorgas-board of distractions for the available men of 30A. Week after week they come in droves. What's a girl to do?

My advice: DO NOT try to compete with these women! You cannot win. They are like a perfect storm of hotness and crazy that rolls in on a Sunday and leaves on a Saturday. Just continue to be your rockin' self at all times. Eventually, a discerning man will have an appetite for local flavor! Also, remember that as go the women so go the men. If the beach is a popular vacation destination for hapless hotties, hunky men will surely follow. The boys of summer are sure to show you a good time while the locals have put you on the shelf for the season.

For God's sake, take advantage! Double standards aside; what's good for Gander is good for the Goose. As long as you're single and just out to play, let me recommend a three martini playdate with a cutie from out of town. Please play responsibly! I wouldn't want any STD's or unplanned love children on my conscience.

11. Chapter Eleven

For all of you divorced ladies, I think we'll skip this one!

12. Dress for Success!

Just like in the work place, the way that you dress can often influence your rate of success in the world of dating. I don't want to come off as judgmental, but has anyone else noticed the complete lack of wardrobe etiquette these days? Let me preach for a second. That's right, this is a Come to Mama moment. No matter how much you love your Nike workout shorts, yoga pants, UGGS, tennis shoes and college T-shirts, none of these are appropriate date attire. I know that feeling comfortable is important, but this is the wrong kind of comfy. As I have mentioned, when I'm not skiing or writing, I work in a popular restaurant. This is Ground Zero for date observation. As far as I can tell my friends, we need to establish some rules.

Small towns are often isolated from the cookie-cutter fashion trends being embraced by women everywhere else. This can be a blessing and a curse. On the one hand, you are freer to express yourself in a small town. On the other, you may not always be expressing your best self. Face it, you aren't sixteen- thank God- so don't try to get away with the kind of stuff you did in high school. Here are a few hints to help you express your best self at all times...

1. Leave something to the imagination. Believe it or not, most men still appreciate the art of anticipation. How can you get your hand caught in the jar if all of the cookies are on the table? Keep it fun for both of you,

make him work for a glimpse of what lies beneath. Just give him a taste and, believe me, he will keep coming back for more.

2. Ditch the coverall and the Mumu. Unless you are planning on joining "Farmersonly.com"; please, please, lose the overalls and Birkenstocks. There is literally no uniform in the world that more directly translates to "I have completely given up" than a loosely and fully covered body.

3. Keep it simple. Too fancy can be intimidating, and can often be misread as "high maintenance". Men don't like to feel inadequate or intimidated. In order to avoid this, I like to rock well fitted jeans and heels on the outside, and beyond sexy underthings. There is a purpose to this. I want men to see me as: A) comfortable, B) confident, and C) easy-going. Then, I want them to ask

themselves, “I wonder what she is wearing underneath all that awesome?”

All told, you should really just wear what makes you feel beautiful. You can be super sexy in a gunny sack if that’s what does it for you. True story; I’ve seen t done! It’s all in how you rock it!

13. Gay on the A

As if small town dating weren’t hard enough, try being a homosexual! Actually, let me rephrase. You don’t really have to try to be a homosexual, but make an effort to see it from their point of view. Now if you want try something new… more power to ya! But this chapter is about the plight of all of my single gay friends up and down 30A and in small towns everywhere.

If you thought that the straight dating pool was small, know this, the gay one is barely a puddle. Apart from those ladies that turn into lesbians after one too many

Chardonnays (you know who you are), the list of actual homosexual prospects is short and narrow. The list gets even shorter when you are seeking a relationship with someone who is already out of the closet. It may seem as though everyone available has already dated or hooked up with everyone else. That is because it is true. With so few local prospects, the cat often has a way of making it back.

There are other ridiculous challenges to being gay on the “A”. Homophobia is still rampant in this world, and small towns tend to be the perfect breeding ground for this ailment. People simply do not accept what they do not understand. This is in no way an excuse for being small minded. I can’t imagine to anguish that one must go through without having any role models to look up to if you aren’t certain about your sexuality. A person may spend their entire life not even capable of fathoming that their sexual orientation is not what they were taught in health class.

Therefore, my gay friends, I encourage you to seize every opportunity for happiness!

When you are gay in a small town, dating a tourist actually *can* be considered “taking you’re A off the A”. Some of these tourists may only ever get the chance to live out loud when they are on vacation. This means that they are usually super discreet about their extra-curricular activities. The point of taking time off the “A” is to enjoy a little privacy and anonymity. If your partner is committed to keeping their private life very private, by all means, go for it!

14.Oh BeHAVE!

On 30A, when a friend asks you how your weekend went, the most appropriate response is often, "Why, what did you hear?" After a typical evening out in a small town, people will likely be talking about where you went, who you danced with, and what you drank before your head ever hits the pillow. When there is not much else to talk about and not much else to do, other people's business can be totally intriguing. Don't let the small town bring you down!

Let's get right down to it. Who really cares what other people have to say about you dancing on tables at the only late night club on the street? It's highly probable that they were either on the table next to you or they wish that they were. In order to assess behavior after a good time, just ask yourself the following:

A). Did you have fun?

B). Did you have a safe ride?

Seriously, please always make sure that the answer to this one " Yes." Good times shouldn't threaten lives!

C). Did you get pregnant or should you take penicillin?

D). Was anyone a casualty of your debauchery? Did you hurt anyone, yourself included, in any way?

If the answers are A: Yes, B: Yes, C: No, and D: No, SUCCESS!!! Go on and give those "concerned citizens" something to talk about! Consider it a public service. Just please remember to always wear under pants when dancing on bars. No matter what you may think, no one wants to see that!

15. Take One for the Team

The same old places, filled with the same old faces can be reassuring. Your good friends and familiar surroundings can be a safe harbor from the storm of singledom. I find that I often crave that sweet reassurance, but reassurances can often create ruts. The same old faces in the same old places can become, for lack of a better term,

BORING! It's only natural to feel this way. No matter how awesome your friends are and no matter how enticing your regular haunts can be there will come a time for change.

Why not shake things up while showcasing your very own brand of "Sporty Spice"? Get your "A" out there and join a team! Every town- even the smallest one- has a sporting organization. An adult sport/social league is a fantastic way to get out there and make new friends while bypassing the bar. Or at the very least a way get your blood pumping and some color in your cheeks before you and your teammates head out for a celebratory cocktail.

You don't have to be a natural athlete to join in on the fun. I promise you, no one wants me to join their baseball team. And golf, well let's just say NEVER! Yet there are plenty of other grown up leagues for everyone. From soccer to dodgeball, volleyball to rugby, there is surely a team out there that will be a perfect fit. Most of these leagues are very social and may also prove to be a pretty good little workout. Never underestimate the amount of energy required to sprint between bases.

Outside of waterskiing, I personally participate in an adult kickball and dodgeball league. Yes, this sounded equally as nerdy in my head. However, my teammates are among the most rad people that I have ever met. Each Wednesday, nearly one hundred adults head out to the field armed with tutus, wigs, Fireball and team spirit. Rainouts sometimes become competitive karaoke- also equally as nerdy in my head, but such a guilty pleasure! Thursday mornings can be a bit fuzzy though, I have heard rumors about girls waking up in jerseys from another team, possibly covered in cheesy tater-tots. These are sometimes the greasy beginnings of adult league love stories! Sexual tension and team drama abound. It's freaking fabulous!!! The friends that I have made by grace of the comradery that comes from teamwork, are so very precious to me. It feels great to spend at least one day a week with a whole team of people who have your back. It is a great way for me to not feel alone in a place that can be desperately lonely. My teammates make me run, make me play, make me laugh, and make me proud. The moments that I have spent with them in both victory and defeat have helped me to define the woman that I chose to be.

If team sports just aren't really your thing, you could always explore a gym membership. I don't care how young and beautiful you are, a little exercise never hurt anyone. And if you're in to health and fitness; where better to meet a like-minded mate? The gym can be a win/win. My only caution: Shy away from that guy making ugly noises as he lifts. And the guy checking out his glutes in the mirror. Trust me on this one... that guy does not want to meet a woman.

16. Ballin' on a Budget

Being a single woman can get very expensive very quickly whether you live in

Mayberry or Manhattan. Bar tabs, dinners, hairdressers, gym memberships and shoes will quickly find their way to demolishing your paycheck. What's a gal to do? We all want to pursue happiness in our own way. It's our constitutional right... right? Worry not, instead allow me to present you a few fun ways to combat fiscal demolition.

1. Host a cookout, or invite friends for dinner at home: Having a pot-luck style get together at your place has several benefits, not the least important of which is privacy. In your own home, you can behave any way you want without worrying about prying eyes. You can let things get downright weird if you want! Why not? You are only among friends. Another benefit is that you can make it BYOB, especially if you provide the eats. This saves *you* a bar tab. Also, house parties happen at HOME. This

eliminates the urge to drive and saves you cab fare. You can help save your friends the same by encouraging a sleepover!

2. Get a bicycle: Bikes are just plain fun. And getting outside while getting some exercise is far less mundane than commuting to your local gym. More to the point; taking advantage of bikes and walking trails and beaches for your daily exercise can save you gym fees. Plus, if you live in a small town, you can save on gas by riding your bike instead of your car. Save money while working on a rockin' body; win/ win.
3. Camping/ RV-ing: Looking to get away for a weekend, but can't stomach the price tag of a hotel? Get out there! You can find a decent tent for under $100 and grab your friends for adventure time. Camping is an awesome way to blow off steam and

feel like you've gone on a small vaycay. Chilling out around the fire, and sleeping under the stars always takes me back to a time when things were simply less complicated. We should all try to take a little time out and howl at the moon. If you are skiddish about tent dwelling, you may want to consider renting an RV. Last year, my girlfriends and I hit the open road for a music festival weekend. We rented an RV that was covered in the Stars and Stripes. One side had a cowboy on a bull and on the other was a giant NASCAR vehicle. Yes, we were VERY sexy. We had hands down the best weekend of my entire life- and I got married on a weekend, so that's saying something. Our adventure felt epic in our cozy little home on wheels. My girls and I spent around two hundred dollars each for a weekend of absolute unadulterated silliness, and it was worth every single dime. It was empowering to learn how to "rough it" on our own. A word of advice though; ALWAYS wear gloves if you're going to attatch the "shitter". That blue tube is really, really nasty, and this piece of advice was learned the hard way!

4. Gau Naturelle: Hair styling and maintenance can cost a pretty penny. If I don't pay close attention, I can find myself spending about two hundred dollars every six weeks. I actually did that this winter when I had a small identity crisis (don't judge, we have all been there!) and died my hair brunette. This may seem a strange choice for a natural blonde, but it was my subtle way of sticking it to the Man. Ex-Man that is, you see, he prefers blondes. Color rebellion aside, I learned very quickly that I couldn't afford to maintain my

stand against the Man. When blonde roots emerge at the crown of a brunette, it looks oddly gray. This is not the statement that I wanted to make! Lesson learned. Now I try to keep it close to natural . This saves me a considerable amount of money, and as a bonus, I recognize myself each time that I look in the mirror. For you brunettes out there who have bleached your tresses, remember that "ombre" hair can be very sexy. Of course this just means that it's cool to grow out your roots, but everything sounds better when you put a French accent on it. For those who may have recently discovered some premature "platinum", I strongly recommend blending it with blonde. Of course, I'm no professional stylist, but I have seen it done and it is super easy to maintain. While it is true that you can't put a price on feeling fabulous, you can keep it within reason. Taking a practical stance toward hair care can buy you at least on extra martini a week. This too can be fabulous, and that is what really matters.

5. Tinder Budget: No, I'm not kidding. If your friends haven't yet staged a "tindervention", going out on a few dates can be an effective way to save a little cash. I personally prefer to go Dutch, but I will never say no to a gentleman insisting upon paying a tab or two. This may sound a bit old fashioned, but sometimes it's nice to be made to feel special. So when that Tinder-dude offers, always accept with a smile and a "thank you". You deserve to be treated once in a while. Just always remember that you don't owe anyone anything just because they offered you dinner. Some guys still believe that dinners entitle them

to some kind of reward. Only go there if that is what *you* want!

*** Footnote: If you ever find yourself in need of a ride and short on cash, flag down a pizza delivery vehicle. I have done this before but only with friends. I wouldn't recommend this as a solo mission. But if you don't mind riding shotgun with pizza on your lap, this can be an effective way to skip on cab fare.***

17.The Double Standard

Earlier on in the guide, I mentioned an existing double standard. And I feel obligated to share some shades on the topic before we continue any further down this road. I didn't chose this moment for any literary purpose, I simply feel that it is a subject that must be addressed before we reach the end of our journey together.

To be thorough, I asked my good friend, Google, to define *dou*ble Stand*ard.* According to my web search, a double standard is a rule that is unfairly applied in different ways to different people or groups. Life is full of double standards. We are introduced to them at such an early age, that we become seemingly immune to them. "Do as I say, not as I do." Do you remember hearing these words from a parent? They usually followed some liberal use of foul language, or possibly a neighborly display of intoxication. Perhaps you felt the sting of a double standard when an older sibling was allowed to stay up late while you were punished for missing your bed time.

The double standard is obviously not just a small town issue, and it goes deeper as we get older. We see it every day! When economically challenged and facing a drug charge- a situation that I would pray none of us will ever know- you are likely to be handed time in prison. The flip side of this standard is that when you are a celebrity facing the same charge you are shuttled off in a limousine to spend twenty-eight days in a cushy rehab.

Even though we are currently in the year 2015, the double standard still applies in our places of work. I'm not referring to the obvious wage inequality here. At work it is not unusual for an assertive woman to be considered a bitch, while a man would simply be considered assertive. A woman with strong leadership skills is considered a nag and an articulate woman is considered to be overly chatty. A man with any of these skills is simply a man who is great at his job.

This brings me, of course, to the real application of the double standard in the wide world of dating. Why is it that a man who dates multiple women is considered to be a "player"? And, further, why is being a "player" a good thing? Male "playership" is a sign that the man is charming, virile, and generally very sexy. Women see him as a man in demand who can chose from multiple possible mates. Here's where it gets unfair. A woman who wants to get in on that kind of action by dating multiple men is considered to be at best a little out of control and at worst a total slut. Why does a woman have to be perceived as desperate for attention while simply behaving in the same manner as her male counterpart? This slutty status is only made worse when a woman finds herself getting played by a player. Nothing makes us question our judgement and character more than falling for someone who was never going to be there to catch you.

Who set these standards, by the way? Why on Earth should we continue to live within their arbitrary confines? I say FORGET the double standard! Live *above* the standards of society and set your own! If you are being responsible in your affairs, then you are accountable only to yourself. Playing around in a responsible and discreet manner does not make you a slut. It makes you a woman who knows what she is looking for and is not afraid to pursue it. Or you may be self-aware enough to recognize that while you desire companionship, you are not quite ready to fall in love.

A word of advice: if you are only out to play, set a strict policy of only hanging with other players. This policy will prevent any confusion that might arise concerning the future of your "relationship". That said, if you are playing the field in search of something more meaningful, a known player will be your emotional downfall. Avoid these men! Even if they approach you claiming a desire to change their prowling ways, take it slowly. A leopard does not change its spots overnight.

Footnote double standard: Why is it art if Miley licks a hammer? Whenever I try it, security escorts me from the Home Depot!

18. G.N.O. aka... What Happened Last Night?

With all of this focus on dating, I fear that I have not given justice to the enormous importance that should be placed upon that age old ritual: The Girls' Night Out. Single, married, parent, or otherwise, your time with the ladies is precious. A great G.N.O. begins with only one motive- To simply go out with your most beloved gal pals, and leave the boys behind. Alright, I meant to leave the boys behind *physically*, however we all know that they will be the main topic of many conversations over the course of the evening!

But really, your girlfriends are your support system. They are your silly. Girls' Night Out should count as your spiritual re-up. When you have a night with the Ladies, you have an opportunity to sing like there is no-one else listening. Karaoke night can be a fun option for this, especially if you can't carry a tune. These nights afford you time to dance like there isn't anyone watching and to celebrate like there is no tomorrow. Your Girls bring out the best in you. You all should bring out the best in each other. If this is not the case, you are hanging out with the wrong group!

Some of the key benefits of a good G.N.O. include:

1. Unabashed silliness.
2. Uncensored venting.
3. Support and understanding from ladies who know what you are going through.
4. Unintentional appeal to potential mates.

Have you ever noticed that the ladies who are just out for a good time together are almost always the most attractive women in the establishment? I know that this may seem like an oxy-moron, but the truth of the matter is, often the best way to find a mate is to not be looking for him at all.

This adage is especially true in a small town. With fewer social outlets and fewer suitors, if you are actively in search of Mr. Right, you are more likely to be perceived as that chick out trolling for love on the regular. Do not be this lady! This lady wreaks of desperation, which we all know is about as appealing to a man as a tub of catfish bait. (If you are from a small town, you may recognize this simile. Catfish bait smalls like dookie!) Fishing for love by just hanging out with the Gals is way more fun, because you all aren't really fishing at all. Really, why just drop in one line when you and the Girls can cast a whole net?

A really great G.N.O. will often result in a series of early morning texts that may read: "What happened last night??" While you all, as a group, try to piece together the history of last night's activities just remember that if you have the general impression of having had a good time, you have been successful! Hopefully you all were safe. Hopefully you all had a blast. Hopefully there were no victims of group debauchery! Who cares if no-one will ever fully recall the whole story? G.N.O. still reigns supreme as a great way to blow off steam and keep it between the Ladies.

19. Oops! I did it Again! The Story of "O" I went and Fell in Love.

Whether or not you have ever been married, by the time we reach adulthood, we have all experienced heartbreak. Having your heart splattered all over your own version of the "A" is a rite of passage. It is what separates the woman from the girl. And it separates the man from the boy.

Growing an adult heart is a slow process, I think. It begins with that first crush who asks Andrea to the Fun Fair instead of you. That boy who chose to take Nikki to the Homecoming dance over you because Nikki actually needed to wear a bra. These little heartbreaks slowly fortify us for that first big one. They help us prepare for that crushing moment that pushes us over the precipice that separates puppy love from the real thing.

When that first real love happens, it can be- and usually is- all consuming. Fueled by passion beyond compare that first real love is tempered not by reason, but by the rapid beating of two untested hearts. If my studies in French Literature have taught me anything, it is that this brand of young love leads inevitably to terrific heartbreak and pain. Ovid states, *"L'amour est une espece de guerre, il n'y a pas de place pour les laches!"* Loosely translated, Ovid was telling us that love is a sort of war. There is no room for the weak. We must invariably fortify our hearts through the folly of our youth in order to withstand the power of the real thing. Love moves constantly from misery to salvation, and back to misery again. You must have some kind of courage to just plain go for it!

It was a special kind of heartbreak that fueled my desire to write this guide. I felt a deep need to celebrate the changes in me for which my pain was the catalyst. This may imply that I am a natural masochist. This may be true. I happen to have an unusually high tolerance for both physical and emotional pain. I wouldn't go so far as to draw a direct reference between myself and Mademoiselle "O" from *The Story of "O"*- whips and irons aren't my thing- but I do find that walking through fire can be regenerative. Like the tall pines that line my precious 30A after a controlled burn, I find myself free to grow anew.

That said; can one fall in love again? Of course! It is not how our hearts get broken. We have already established that everyone has been through that! The key is in how you decide to put the pieces back together. We as a species were never meant to be alone. Our hearts will instinctively seek a mate. Just remember that this time will most definitely be different from the last (although not necessarily better). This is Love's only guarantee. Yet, if it can happen to the likes of me, it can happen for all of us. I 'm not ready to say that I'll ever be ready to revisit wedding bells and white lace, but who knows? Time has a funny way!

****"Three words that became hard to say. I. And Love. And you..." -Avett Brothers****

20. Be the Bad "A"

When I started this writing adventure, I was newly single, completely clueless and very afraid of where my new road would take me. So afraid, in fact, that I didn't even want to step onto the path. This guide began as a conversation that I found myself having over and over again with my single friends. I found that sharing my hilarious new experiences to be extremely satisfying, and I made them laugh, which made me laugh right along with them. I began to understand that being thirty something and single requires a very open mind and a big sense of humor. Basically, my situation was so sad that it was funny. I was like one of those dogs that are so ugly you can't help but find that they are adorable. I was adorably pathetic, and I began to convince myself that I could fix my situation in a series of small steps.

This was untrue. I now find myself unsure of whether or not I need to fix anything. Here is what I know to be true: I will never be the woman that I was before I wrote this guide. The other truth is that I don't *want* to be that woman anymore! What I have discovered on this adventure is that this small town has made a badass out of me.

The accountability of local eyes constantly following me has pushed me to edit myself into the best version of me. And now I am a badass. Now I am free to be exactly myself and love- even the broken bits. I solemnly vow to all of you that I will continue to discover who I am, to love who I choose to love, and be the person that I choose to be!

In Totem: I believe in each and every one of us; the career woman, the Martha, the Lindsay and the Drew, and the somewhere-in-between. Each of us shares a shade of Grayton and we need to hold it, nurture it, and never settle for less than happy! Our shades are ever changing. Who really knows what life will bring? Be Thirty Shades of YOU and rock it solid ladies! I love you all. You all inspire me each and every day! Go out, get it on and get it all!

30 Shades of GrAyton

Scribble the Shades of Your

Personal Journey

(Don't leave out the good bits!!!)

60275358R00051

Made in the USA
Charleston, SC
29 August 2016